DUDLEY SCHOOLS
LIBRARY SERVICE

Going places available in hardback
People on holiday

Going places available in paperback
Finding the way
How places change
People at work
People on the move
Town and countryside
Where people shop

Acknowledgements

Illustrations by Tessa Richardson-Jones
Photographs by Zul Mukhida except for: pp. 10t, 11t Mary Evans/
Bruce Castle Museum; pp. 10b, 11b Mary Evans Picture Library; pp. 14t
Michael Marten, 15tl US Geographical Survey, 15b Soames
Summerhays, 23tr Kent and Donna Danner, 23b Peter Menzel, Science
Photo Library; pp. 14b Paul Harris, 15tr Victoria Keble-Williams, 26b
Roger Mear, 27 Martha Holmes, Royal Geographical Society; pp. 16l
Tim Garrod, 16r Jayne Knights, 17m Oliver Cockell, 26t Tim Garrod, Zul
Colour Library; p. 17t Peter Arkell, Impact; pp. 17b, 21, 22, 23m, 24b
Jenny Matthews; pp. 23tl, 24t Mark Edwards, Still Pictures.

The author and publisher would like to thank the staff and pupils
of Balfour Infant School, Brighton.

A CIP record for this book is available from
the British Library.

ISBN 0-7136-6365-0

First paperback edition published 2002
First published in hardback in 1995 by
A & C Black Publishers Ltd
37 Soho Square, London, W1D 3QZ
www.acblack.com

© 1995 A & C Black Publishers Ltd
A CIP record for this book is available from
the British Library.

A & C Black uses paper produced with elemental chlorine-free pulp,
harvested from managed sustainable forests.

Typeset in Rowland Phototypesetting Ltd,
Bury St Edmunds, Suffolk
Printed in Belgium by Proost International Book Production

going places

How places change

Barbara Taylor

Illustrations by Tessa Richardson-Jones
Photographs by Zul Mukhida and Jenny Matthews

Contents

A & C Black · London

Changes around you

Do you know how old your school is? Perhaps there is a date written on the building somewhere. Can you find out how the school has changed since it was built? Have there been any changes to the school in the last year?

Finding out about buildings such as your school, will help you to discover how your local area has changed. If your school is very old, it means that there were children living in the area long ago. You might be able to find some photographs showing what the school used to look like.

If your school is new, it might have replaced an old school which has been demolished or damaged by a fire. Or it may have been built for the children of new families moving into the area.

This is St Luke's junior school in Brighton. The school was built in 1903.

How would you change your school to make it a better place? Ask your friends about the changes they would like to make too. You could draw a chart to show what you find out.

I'd like a special computer room.

These children are looking at the changes to the buildings, roads and shops in their local town. Here are some of the changes they spotted.

old church
being mended

new road layout

old houses being
knocked down

new superstore
being built

new playground

The children recorded the changes on a map of the town. They have made up some simple pictures, called symbols, to show each change. For example, a traffic light stands for a new road layout.

A list called a key on the edge of the map explains what the symbols stand for.

Do you think the changes made to this town are good changes? Why do you think the changes have been made?

What changes might the children have seen on a walk in the countryside?

Finding out about change

Have you ever wondered what your local area looked like long ago? How do you think it has changed? Your local library should have old photographs, postcards and maps showing what your area used to look like.

This tram line was opened in Enfield in 1905. Nowadays, electric trams are making a comeback because they cause less pollution and can avoid traffic jams.

This is Eastbourne seafront about 100 years ago. How would the clothing, transport and hotels look different today?

You could also find out about the changes to your local area by talking to people who have lived in the area for a long time. What questions could you ask them to help you find out about the changes? Here are some ideas.

This street in London was badly damaged by a bomb during the Second World War. Are there any places in your local area which were bombed during the war?

This picture was taken in Wiltshire in 1937. The ploughmen and horses are having lunch. In those days, lots of farmers still used horses for heavy farm work such as ploughing.

Has the town or village got bigger or smaller?

Is there more or less countryside nearby?

How have the shops changed?

When was the railway station built?

Are there any big new factories?

How many people lived in your area 50 years ago?

Have any factories closed down?

Is there more traffic than there used to be?

Spot the changes

Look carefully at these two pictures of Crabtree Village.
One picture shows the village as it was in 1900 and one
is a modern picture of the village. Is Crabtree bigger or
smaller than it was in 1900?
How has Crabtree changed? Look carefully
at the houses, roads, traffic and shops.

(The answers are at the bottom of the next page.)

Crabtree Village, 1900

Crabtree Village, 1995

Answers:

1 Crabtree is much bigger than it was and it has a lot more roads.

2 Some old houses have been knocked down and new houses have been built in other parts of the village.

3 The old school has been demolished and a new school has been built in a different place.

4 The blacksmith's has been turned into a museum.

5 There are a lot of new buildings, including a cinema, supermarket and police station.

6 There is less farmland and green spaces although there is a new park on the outskirts of the village.

7 The village now has a railway station.

Changes to the landscape

Places can change because of natural forces such as the sea or the wind, which alter the shape of the land, building it up in some places and eating into it in others. There are also powerful forces under the ground which cause earthquakes and volcanoes.

Most of the changes to the landscape happen very slowly over hundreds or millions of years, so you can't see them taking place. Some changes though, such as earthquakes, happen suddenly, without any warning.

Look carefully at these pictures of changes to the landscape in different parts of the world. Which changes have taken a long time and which happened suddenly?

This tall pillar of rock, called the Old Man of Hoy, is 137m high. It formed when waves cut through the sandstone rocks which joined it to the cliffs.

In the Grand Canyon, in North America, the Colorado River has carved away the rocks to make a valley which is 1.6km deep.

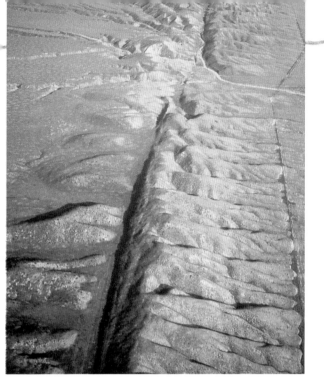

In the Namib desert, in Africa, the wind has blown the sand into huge heaps called dunes.

The San Andreas fault in California, USA, is a huge crack in the earth's crust. Strong forces under the ground make the rocks on either side of the crack move, and this can cause earthquakes.

Boiling hot liquid rocks, called lava, pour from the Kilauea Volcano in Hawaii, covering the mountain with a new layer of rock.

What shape is the land in your area? Have you noticed any changes? If you live near the sea, there might be an area of coastline which is being eaten away by the waves. Or you might live near to a river which has burst its banks because of heavy rain. What other changes could you look out for?

Changes made by people

One of the main reasons for change is that there are more people in the world. This means that there are more houses, workplaces, shops and schools and fewer countryside areas. It also means that more land needs to be farmed to grow food.

Another reason for change is to do with the way buildings are designed and the building materials that are used. Today, many cities are a mixture of old and new buildings.

In this area of Madeira, all the available space has been used to grow crops.

Look at this picture of Chinatown in Singapore. Which buildings are old and which are new?

Many places changed a lot when old factories or industries closed down.

Another reason for change is to do with transport. Many roads have been widened to make room for more cars, buses and lorries. There are also a lot more airports and railway stations than there were years ago.

This coal mine in South Hetton, Cleveland, closed in 1977. How do you think this affected the people who live there?

This area of docklands in London was left to decay for many years. In the 1980s, new offices and banks were built on the land.

The Channel Tunnel takes people from England to France by train. Waterloo station, in London, had to be extended to make room for the special trains.

Many places change a lot when valuable things such as coal, oil and diamonds are discovered in the ground. In the 1800s, parts of California changed overnight when gold was discovered in the rocks. Empty countryside turned into bustling towns as people poured into the area to make their fortune.

This is a picture of a place where gold has been discovered by a miner called Jethro. He is just galloping off to tell people the exciting news.

How do you think the place will change now? Where will the gold diggers live? Where will they get their food, water and clothes? How will they get their gold to a bank for safe keeping?

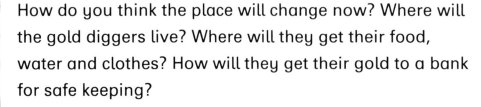

Draw a map of Jethro town a year from now. Make up symbols for things like the houses, the mine, the bank and the roads. What will happen to Jethro town when the gold runs out?

Planning for change

Most towns and cities employ a team of people, called a town council, who make decisions about the changes made to their town.

The town council in Rose Town has voted to spend some money improving the town. Here is a list of the changes the council would like to make and how much each one costs. The money in Rose Town is called pitars.

shopping centre
– 150 pitars

park – 20 pitars

new school – 100 pitars

cinema – 40 pitars

library – 25 pitars

leisure centre – 70 pitars

hospital – 200 pitars

Look carefully at this map of Rose Town. The council has only got 300 pitars to spend. Which changes do you think they should make?

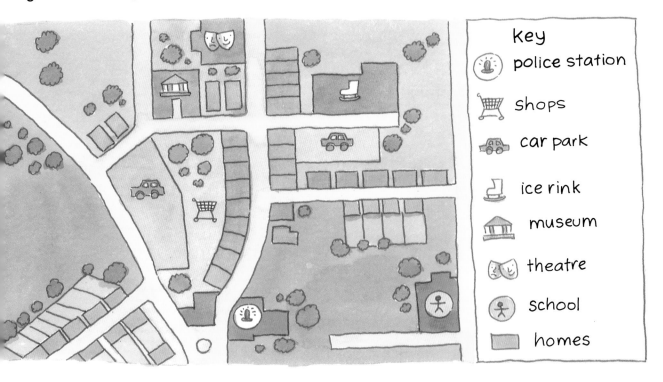

key

🚨 police station

🛒 shops

🚗 car park

🍨 ice rink

🏛 museum

🎭 theatre

🧍 school

▭ homes

Once the changes have been decided, a person called a town planner thinks up ideas for where to put the new buildings and parks. Imagine that you are a town planner in Rose Town.

Draw a map of the town, and mark on the changes you would like to make. Where do you want the new buildings or parks to go? Think about where people live and how they will get to the new buildings. Will the town need to build some new roads?

This man is planning a new town for refugees returning to El Salvador.

Most of the time, change is planned and things happen gradually. But sometimes, changes are very sudden and cannot be planned for. Sudden changes are often due to natural disasters, such as a flood or an earthquake, or they may be caused by war.

Look carefully at these photographs of places around the world. Do you think the changes taking place have been planned? Have you seen any of these changes in your area?

Building shanty town houses in Sao Luis, Brazil.

Demolishing towerblocks in Hackney, London.

Building a new road in Mexico City, Mexico.

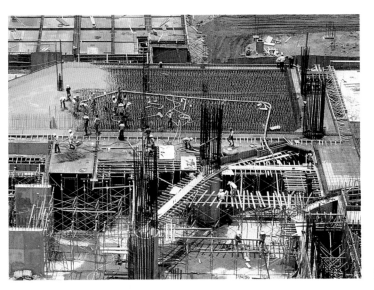

Flooding in Estes Park, Colorado, USA.

Building an hotel in Columbo, Sri Lanka.

Earthquake damage to a freeway in Oakland, California, USA.

Green changes

The changes that people make to places can affect the environment. How is the environment changing in your area? Is there much pollution from factories, power stations or cars? Are there any empty buildings which have been rebuilt and put to new uses?

How could you change your environment to make your area a better place to live?

These children are planting tree seedlings in Sri Lanka.

Houses in this street have been demolished to make way for a new motorway.

I'd like to make the town centre free of cars.

I'd turn the wasteground into a park.

We could build a wildlife area.

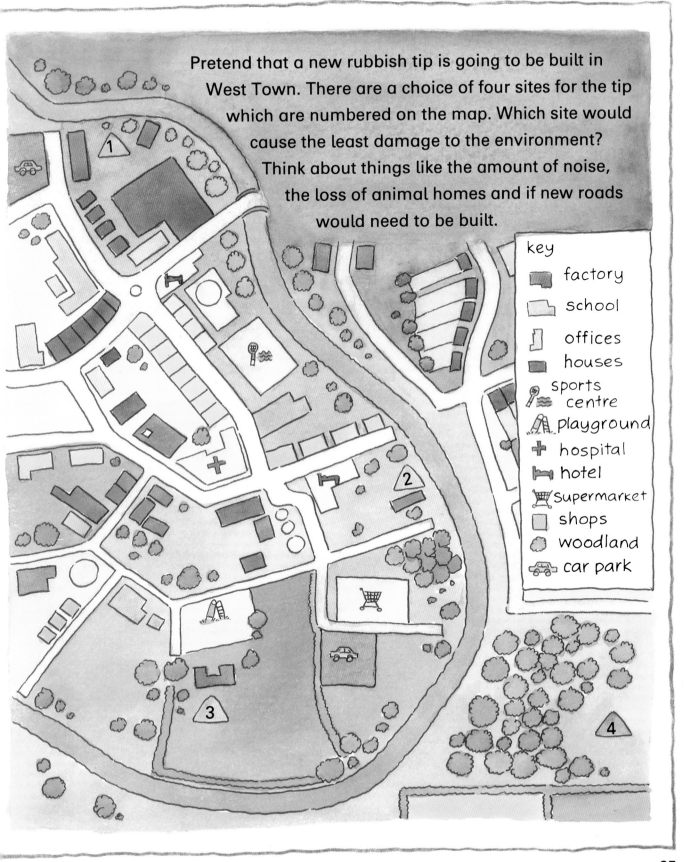

Pretend that a new rubbish tip is going to be built in West Town. There are a choice of four sites for the tip which are numbered on the map. Which site would cause the least damage to the environment? Think about things like the amount of noise, the loss of animal homes and if new roads would need to be built.

key

factory
school
offices
houses
sports centre
playground
hospital
hotel
supermarket
shops
woodland
car park

Then, now and tomorrow

When people first began to settle in places and build villages and towns, they could choose where they wanted to build them. Nowadays, the world is getting very crowded and more land is being used to grow food and to provide people with homes and workplaces.

People crossing the road in Tokyo, Japan.

One of the few places on Earth which has not been changed much by people is Antarctica. It is a long way from any other land and has a very cold climate. Most of the land is covered in ice and snow and only animals such as penguins, whales and seals visit in the summer.

A leopard seal in Antarctica.

At the moment the climate is unsuitable for people, but scientists are developing the technology to live and work there inside warm, air-conditioned buildings. Many people think Antarctica should be left alone and that people shouldn't change it. What do you think?

McMurdo Station in Antarctica.

If you were a time traveller who could go forward into the future, what sort of changes do you think you'd see in fifty years time? Or one hundred years time?

Index

For parents and teachers
More about the ideas in this book

Pages 6/9 'How places change' is a potentially huge subject. Using the school as a starting point will help to focus the attention of the children on small changes that affect their own lives.

Pages 10/13 Expanding outwards from the school to the local area allows topics such as transport, shops, work, farming, homes and the supply of goods and services to be introduced. Encourage the children to record changes to their local area and to express opinions about the changes they see.

Pages 14/15 The shape of the Earth's surface has changed over thousands of millions of years due to the movement of molten rock within the planet and the erosive power of wind and water on the surface. Rivers and coasts are two places where children can easily see natural changes at work.

Pages 16/19 Differences between town and countryside locations should provide useful discussion points. Reasons for changes to places are often linked to population growth as well as developments in building designs and transport. The development of gold rush towns is a good example of how places change overnight.

Pages 20/21 These pages introduce the concept of budgeting and voting for change. Individuals in a community can make a difference to the way a place changes.

Pages 22/23 Catastrophic events such as wars and earthquakes often force unwelcome changes on places. The economics of change is also a factor, since changes have to be paid for.

Pages 24/25 In developed countries, the environmental impact of change is becoming an increasingly important factor in business, but taking care of the environment can be expensive.

Pages 26/27 Originally, people changed places to help themselves survive the climate, grow food and defend themselves from attack. Nowadays, change has a lot to do with economics and design as well as survival.

Things to do

Going places provides starting points for all kinds of cross-curricular work based on geography and the environment, looking at your locality and at the wider world.

How places change explores the reasons for change and examines the relationships between people and the main physical and human features of their environment. Here are some ideas for follow-up activities to extend the ideas further.

1 Making a book of the history of the school is a useful way of investigating kinds of changes and the reasons they occur. What evidence of change can the children find? Are there any coal sheds or air raid shelters in the playground? Are the toilets separated from the school building? Was there once a different entrance for boys and girls? If the school is a new one, children could think about what changes might happen in the future.

2 Drama activities could be developed from debates or public inquiries about environmental change. The children could discuss local issues as well as global issues such as deforestation, acid rain, over-fishing and global warming.

3 Find out about the development of real gold rush towns in places such as California or Australia. How quickly did towns spring up? What sort of housing and transport was available in remote mining areas? What are these places like today?

4 Write a letter to someone who has been away from the local area for a long time, telling them about the changes that have taken place. Draw a map of your area and mark on the most important changes.

5 Investigate the way rivers change the landscape. Why do young rivers have V-shaped valleys? Why do older rivers meander across flat floodplains? Why do deltas form where rivers meet the sea? Coastal features such as beaches, bays and headlands provide an alternative source of investigation.

6 Imagine that you are a time-traveller and make up a story about travelling backwards and forwards in time. What kind of changes would you notice happening to shops, houses, transport and industries?

7 Draw a time-line to show the changes in building design. How did building design change as new materials were discovered? When was the first skyscraper built? The children could make up designs for buildings of the future.

8 Look out for newspaper reports of natural disasters such as floods, earthquakes and volcanic eruptions. Find the places on a map of the world. Encourage the children to think about how these disasters affect both the physical landscape and the lives of the people. What sort of help do the people need?

9 Draw a map of the locality, incorporating all the changes which would make it an ideal place to live. Are there any existing buildings or facilities that you would suggest demolishing?

10 Interview a town planner on the local council and ask about changes planned for the local area. Are there any plans for new motorways, by-passes, shopping centres or cycle lanes? Are there any derelict houses that could be put to better use? Is the council planning to make changes in the goods and services it provides? Do they have the money to make the changes they feel are needed?

11 Make up some 'spot the difference' quiz pictures to show how places change. Choose places from different locations, such as a seaside town, a farming village, a big city, a new town and a tourist development.